Sweet Dreams
and Monsters

Sweet Dreams and Monsters

A Beginner's Guide to Dreams and Nightmares
and Things That Go Bump under the Bed

By PETER MAYLE   Illustrated by ARTHUR ROBINS

HARMONY BOOKS/NEW YORK

Published by Harmony Books, a division of Crown Publishers, Inc.,
225 Park Avenue South, New York, New York 10003,
and represented in Canada by the Canadian MANDA Group

HARMONY and colophon are trademarks of Crown Publishers, Inc.
Manufactured in Belgium

Library of Congress Cataloging-in-Publication Data

Mayle, Peter.
Sweet dreams and monsters.
Summary: Explains what happens when we sleep, how daytime experiences can affect our dreams, and different kinds of dreams and nightmares.
1. Dreams—Juvenile literature.   2. Nightmares—Juvenile literature.
[1. Dreams.   2. Nightmares] I. Robins, Arthur, ill. II. Title.
BF1091.M37   1986   154.6′3   86-7551
ISBN 0-517-55972-2

10 9 8 7 6 5 4 3 2 1
FIRST EDITION

Do you remember the night when there was a monster cockroach hiding under your bed? The one with shark's teeth, long hairy legs, and a zap gun?

He crawled out from under the bed, licked his lips, and rubbed his back legs together, making a loud scratchy sound. He crawled up on the bed. He came closer and closer. He got so close you could almost touch him. His great big mouth, with great big teeth, was just about to bite off your toes for a snack and save the rest of you for lunch. There was nothing you could do, when all of a sudden . . .

You woke up.

Boy, were you scared! One more second and he would have been nibbling your big toe and licking his lips and rubbing his hairy legs together, thinking about lunch. And even after you checked under the bed and all you found were your slippers—even then, your bedroom felt different in the dark. Not the usual friendly place, but scary, because it seemed so real. That cockroach was *there*.

And yet, it was just a dream. A bad dream. Or, to give a bad dream its proper name, a nightmare.

Now, everything is scarier when you don't understand it. We're going to help you understand your dreams: the good ones as well as the bad ones, the forgotten dreams, the cheese-and-pickle-and-ice-cream dreams, the daydreams, and the dream machine that can tell what's going on inside your head while you sleep.

By the time we finish, you will be a dream expert. And your bedroom will once again be the friendly place it really is.

Free Movies Every Night

Everybody dreams. Mothers and fathers, sisters and brothers, teachers, astronauts, movie stars, your best friend, the queen of England, the president of the United States, even cats and dogs.

And they dream every night wherever they are sleeping—in their beds, in their space capsules, in their palaces, in the desert, in the jungle, in tents in the forest, in ships at sea, in trains and in planes and in dog baskets. If you could count them, there are millions and millions and millions of dreams being dreamed every night of the year.

You dream every night, too. You dreamed last night, and you will dream again tonight. The chances are you can't remember last night's dreams, because one of the many odd and interesting things about dreaming is that we forget most of our dreams. One minute you can be fast asleep in the middle of a great dream adventure, the next minute, when you wake up, the dream is gone. Nothing. You may remember you were dreaming, but you can't remember what it was you were dreaming about.

Was it being a tightrope walker in the circus? Was it having your own personal milk-shake factory? Was it meeting a talking cat? Was it having the world's first supersonic flying bed? Who knows? Whatever it was, it vanished the second you woke up. That's how it is most nights with most dreams.

Night after night this can happen, sometimes week after week. And then, just when you are wondering if you will ever remember another dream, you wake up one morning and remember *everything* that you dreamed while you were sleeping, just as if you had gone to the movies. And in a way, your dream seems even more real than the movies. Because unlike the movies, where you can only see and hear what's going on, with dreams you can sometimes smell and feel what's happening as well.

The trouble is that you never know exactly when you are going to remember one of your dreams, so it always takes you by surprise. If it's a good dream you get a nice surprise. If it's a nightmare, you get a nasty shock that can stay with you all day and right through to bedtime. (Those are the nights when you keep the light on and check *very* carefully under the bed before you get in!)

It would be great if we could choose our dreams, just like we choose television programs or movies, but we can't do that. We can't even tell in advance if we're going to remember one of our dreams, so we never know when we go to bed what's going to be showing that night. All we know for sure is that we will be dreaming.

How can we be so sure? Because of an amazing machine that can actually measure your dreams, from the moment they start until the moment they stop.

The Part of You
That Almost Never Sleeps

You probably think that when you go to sleep, all of you goes to sleep. Arms and legs and eyes and ears and nose and stomach, all taking a rest after a busy day of being awake. And it's true that some parts of you do go to sleep. But parts of you don't, and one of these is the part that does all your thinking: your brain.

Even though your brain doesn't make a humming noise or light up in your head like a Christmas tree when it is thinking, it does send out messages that say it's busy. These messages are called brain waves, and somebody not too long ago invented a special machine that can measure these brain waves. The machine can't tell *what* it is that your brain is thinking, but it can tell *when* it's thinking.

Thanks to this dream machine, we now know a lot about dreaming that we never knew before. We know that little babies dream when they're only eight months old. We know that dreaming doesn't stop as you get older, and you will still be having dreams when you're ninety-nine. We know that dreaming is as natural as breathing. We even know how often most people dream each night and how long each dream lasts.

Of course, not everybody dreams exactly the same way at exactly the same time. But let's imagine that you took the dream machine to bed one night. This is what it might tell you the next morning.

A Busy Night in
Your Head

When you first went to sleep, you were very tired, and so was your brain. In fact, both of you were fast asleep for about an hour. Then, while the rest of you was sleeping, your brain woke up and started thinking, not for very long, but for eight or nine minutes. That was your first dream.

After that, your brain had a rest for an hour and a half or so before the next dream. This dream was longer, about nineteen minutes.

And so it goes on through the night. The rest periods stay the same, at about an hour and a half, but the longer you sleep the longer your dreams last. The third dream is for more than twenty minutes. The fourth, for nearly thirty minutes. The fifth dream is even longer, and lasts until you wake up.

If you could get up and check the machine, you would see just how busy your brain had been during the night, getting busier and busier as you got closer to waking up. You might have had as many as five dreams, lasting (if you added them all up) for more than two hours.

Were they sweet dreams? Were they nightmares? Did you meet the giant cockroach or the talking cat or the Man in the Moon? And why did you dream the way you did?

It often depends on what's been happening to you during the day.

The Daytime You and
The Nighttime You

You can't see both of them when you look in the mirror, but there are really two of you.

The one you know best is the daytime you, which is kept busy during the day going to school, playing with friends, watching television, walking the dog, eating and drinking and learning to do handstands without falling over, and generally taking care of the dozens of things that have to be done in between getting up and going to bed. It's busy. It's often so busy that there just isn't time to pay attention to everything that's going on around you.

Or at least, that's what you think. But it's amazing what you do notice without realizing it. In the same way that you can look straight ahead and still see out of the corner of your eye, your mind can be busy doing one thing and still—out of the corner of your mind's eye—be taking in a lot more.

You just don't have the time to think about it all during the day. But when you go to sleep, the nighttime you takes over. And there's plenty of time to think about everything that happened during the day, not just what you were concentrating on. All the things you were too busy to notice at the time come out of storage in the back of your mind, and the nighttime you starts to think about them.

That's why you sometimes wake up and find yourself thinking hard about yesterday instead of today. And then you understand that the kind of day you have often has a lot to do with the kind of night you have.

Let's take a good day. You took a really tough test at school and you did so well the teacher called you professor. You got home to find that your Great Aunt Minnie—the one you thought forgot your birthday—remembered after all and sent you a terrific present. Then you ate your favorite food for dinner and there wasn't time to do the dishes because you had to meet your best friend to go to the movies.

Well, after a good day like that, you might remember it all over again in your sleep and have a whole night of good dreams.

But the opposite can happen, too. Let's say you received the lowest score on a test at school. There was a caterpillar in your sandwich at lunchtime. You fell down and skinned your knee, and the other kids laughed at you. And when you got home, your sister borrowed your bicycle without asking, the dog chewed up your new sneakers, and it was macaroni and cheese for dinner.

A day like that also causes dreams, and they aren't much fun.

It's easy to understand how this happens, because those dreams are just like replays of the best parts or the worst parts of the day before. You could call them memory dreams, because they are night-time reminders of things you did. But you can also dream about things you haven't done—future dreams—and they can seem every bit as real as memory dreams.

Future dreams can be more surprising, more exciting, scarier or funnier than your ordinary every night dream. In the future *anything* can happen.

The question is, what makes you dream about the future? After all, you don't know much about it except that it doesn't start until tomorrow. Why should it suddenly come creeping into your dreams tonight?

The answer is hidden away in that part of your brain you have just read about—the part which stores up a lot of thinking while the rest of you is busy. And it's not just thinking about what happened yesterday or what's happening today, it's also thinking about what's going to happen tomorrow as well.

If tomorrow seems like it's going to be fun, that part of your brain will be looking forward to it. If tomorrow seems like it's going to be horrible, that part of your brain will be worrying about it.

Either way, you are usually too busy taking care of today to spend too much time on tomorrow—until you go to sleep. Then all the hopes and the worries and the thoughts that have been kept in storage turn up as dreams. And what dreams they can be! Just to give you an idea, we'll take a look at *all* the different kinds.

The Family of Dreams

Dreams, like people, can be long or short, friendly or frightening, sad or funny, boring or exciting. As you can imagine, with everybody in the world dreaming every night of the year, there are so many dreams going on that to describe them all would take a book as big as your bed. So what we're going to do instead is tell you about the dreams you are most likely to have. Are you sure you're wide awake? Then here goes.

The Forgotten Dream

This is the most common dream of all. When you wake up in the morning, you're pretty sure you've been dreaming about *something*, but what was it? There was no beginning, there was no end, and nothing was clear. It was just like shadows passing through your head, or watching ghosts through the wrong end of a telescope. You may think you imagined it all, but you didn't. It was a forgotten dream.

The Memory Dream

This one is the opposite of the forgotten dream. Memory dreams are the ones you can remember, which is sometimes great and sometimes not so good. What happens is that your dream takes you back to what you did, or saw, or felt during the day—but often it comes out differently. So if you had a good day, you might have an even better dream: two birthday parties instead of one, or riding to the beach in a spaceship instead of a car. Of course, a bad day can give you a worse dream, but we hope you don't have too many of those.

The Future Dream

You already know a little about future dreams. They're started off by thoughts that you have during the day. Not ordinary, everyday thoughts, but ones that are especially important.

Will they be good or bad? It depends on whether you're excited about the future and looking forward to it, or worried and wishing you could cancel tomorrow because you know you're not going to enjoy it. (Or even worse, you know you're going to hate it.)

You probably have your own special favorite days and horrible days. Christmas might be at the top of your favorite days list, while a trip to the dentist tops your horrible days list.

The night before Christmas you might be so excited you almost don't get to sleep. But when you do, what wonderful dreams you have—of parties and staying up late and so many presents that Santa has to make three trips down the chimney!

The night before the dentist, you can't help wishing that you could hide your teeth somewhere and not have to go. Or else that it was him in the dentist's chair and you playing with all the gadgets. But when you fall asleep and dream, it's always you in the chair, and the dentist (who's really very nice) seems to be doing his best to climb right inside your mouth.

But that's the way future dreams are. Bigger (and sometimes worse) than real life.

Dreams from the Screen

When the movie has finished and the television set is turned off, the pictures may leave the screen, but they stay in your head. You remember them when you're awake, and you remember them in your sleep. But there's one big difference. In your dreams, you're not just watching what's happening on the screen, you're part of what's happening as well. When the Two-headed Purple Demon from outer space is trying to escape from the Intergalactic Flying Squad, you're *there*, at the controls, your finger on the button that will release the giant green jelly bomb and put an end to him once and for all.

Sometimes it's you who's being chased. When the Haunted Hamburger comes after you, dripping with relish and a hundred times bigger than any hamburger you've ever seen, you run and you run and you still can't get away from him. And then he starts to fire jet-propelled french fries at you!

It only takes a couple of dreams like that before you decide that maybe it's better not to watch scary movies or television shows or read scary books just before you go to bed.

King-size Dreams

Every once in a while, you wake up after a dream that felt like it lasted all night and you remember every second of it. This kind of dream feels so real that even after you've woken up you're not quite sure it was a dream. Maybe someone *did* give you all of Disneyland. Maybe you really *are* the only person in the history of the world who can fly. Maybe your friend the dentist *did* tell you to eat more ice cream. It takes some time before you're absolutely positively sure that it was only a dream. But it was fun while it lasted!

The king-size bad dream—the one that wakes you up in the middle of the night sometimes—is the nightmare. Beetles the size of trucks coming out of the closet! Trapped in a swimming pool full of strained spinach! Exploding chocolate cookies! Being eaten alive by the vacuum cleaner! They seem real—sometimes so real that you sit up in the middle of the night and find you've almost jumped out of your pajamas. It's great when you realize that it didn't really happen, but it can make you frightened of swimming pools and chocolate cookies for quite some time.

Dreams That Come True

Once upon a time there was a very old man who had a dream about a big tiger. In his dream, the tiger followed him home from the supermarket. The old man was very scared, so he locked his door and went to bed. But then the tiger jumped in through the window, and he came up to the old man and he bit him hard on the toe. He bit him so hard that the old man woke up. And do you know what had happened? He really had been bitten on the toe—by his false teeth. They dropped out while he was sleeping.

And then there was a little girl who dreamed that she had a hairy chest that was making funny noises every time she touched it. And when she woke up, she found her cat fast asleep on her chest and purring.

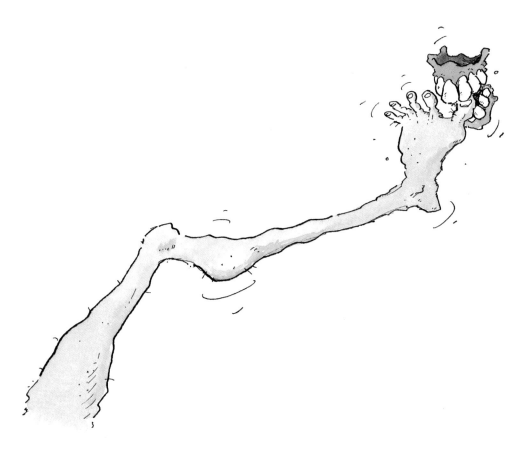

There are hundreds of different dreams like this, started off by something you can feel or hear in your sleep—a thunderstorm, the telephone ringing in another room, the sound of an airplane flying over the house, the blankets falling off the bed and making you dream you're at the coldest part of the North Pole. What makes them different from other dreams is that your brain picks up something that is really happening and makes it part of a dream.

Sometimes, what's really happening isn't going on outside you; it's going on inside. Have you ever been to a birthday party and eaten too much of everything? You went to sleep, but your stomach didn't. It was too full, and it ached. In fact, it was feeling so stuffed it was sending messages up to your brain. And your brain turned those messages into dreams which made you feel bad. (We call those cheese-and-pickle-and-ice-cream dreams, because it's a mixture that most stomachs find hard to take without complaining.)

So you can see that not all dreams are caused by what you're thinking. They can be caused by cats and planes and false teeth and pickles.

Daydreams

The daydream is the only dream you can have without going to sleep, and because you're awake, you can choose what you dream about. So it's not surprising that daydreams are some of the best dreams you can have.

And why do you have them? To escape from what's going on around you! It could be during a long boring car trip when there's not much to see and you're tired of counting license plates from different states. It could be at school when the class seems to be going on for ten times longer than usual. It could be when you just don't want to think about tomorrow. In other words, you have daydreams when you want to think about something more interesting or more fun than whatever it is you're supposed to be thinking about.

Grown-ups are not too sure they like daydreams—at least, not when you have them. They say things like "Why are you wasting your time daydreaming?" and "Stop daydreaming and eat your string beans!" The funny thing is, when grown-ups have daydreams (which they do just as much as you do), they call it thinking or using their imaginations. And they're right. When artists and writers and inventors have daydreams, the results can be wonderful pictures or ideas for books or new gadgets.

Daydreams are short vacations from real life. Enjoy them while they last.

Monsters: Keep Out
A Bedroom Checklist

If you know for certain that there is absolutely nowhere in your bedroom for a twenty-five-foot crocodile to hide, the chances are you won't dream about being bitten by one. The same goes for ghosts, small green men from Mars, spiders, man-eating blobs, or that mean-looking dog who lives down the street.

What you need is a bedroom inspection, and a bedroom inspector to help you. Any grown-up will do fine, but your best bet is your mom or dad, because they know all the hiding places in your bedroom.

- The first place to check is under the bed. Make a complete search with a flashlight, and be sure to look under the covers right down to the foot of the bed.
- Check behind the curtains.
- Look in the closets, and double-check that dark corner where you once thought you saw something spooky.
- Check the place where you keep your toys. If they live in a box, close the lid tightly so they can't jump out even if they want to.
- Now you can get into bed and relax. Snuggle down, close your eyes, sleep tight. And sweet dreams.